SURVIVAL NOTES FOR TEENS

INSPIRATION FOR THE EMOTIONAL JOURNEY

BY
ROBERT STOFEL

Ambassador Books, Inc.
Worcester • Massachusetts

Library of Congress Cataloging-in-Publication Data

Stofel, Robert, 1962-
  Survival notes for teens : inspiration for the emotional journey / by Robert Stofel.
      p. cm.
  ISBN 1-929039-26-3 (pbk.)
  1. Christian teenagers--Religious life. 2. Christian teenagers--Conduct of life. I. Title.

  BV4531.3.S763 2004
  248.8'3--dc22

                              2004020050

Published in the United States by Ambassador Books, Inc.,
91 Prescott Street, Worcester, Massachusetts 01605 • (800) 577-0909

Printed in the United States of America.
For current information about all titles from Ambassador Books, Inc.,
visit our website at: www.ambassadorbooks.com.

Dedicated with love and affection
to my teenage daughter, Sloan

Also by Robert Stofel:

Survival Notes for Graduates:
Inspiration for the Ultimate Journey

CONTENTS

ACKNOWLEDGEMENTS

I thank Ambassador Books for their dedication and determination. They enhanced the book with their heart and soul.

Thanks to my wife, Jill, who kept me encouraged along the way.

Thanks to my two daughters, Blair and Sloan, who lived through half of the advice in this book and survived.

Thanks to Hickory Hills Community Church for all of your support and encouragement.

Thanks to my friends in Franklin, Tennessee and Decatur, Alabama. You know who you are. I love you dearly.

INTRODUCTION

Imagine you are stranded on a deserted island in the Pacific Ocean. All you possess is a small knife that shapes and cuts and cleans what you need to survive. It prepares that lone fish that takes hours to catch and minutes to eat. It provides security and a good night's rest—at least in theory. Because when the bushes rustle, making a mysterious noise, the knife is there. Its safety reflects the moon on its blade.

And living in the open air on an island will expose you for who you really are. Do you have the character and the bravery to survive? And Scripture says, "The word of God is full of living power. It is sharper than the sharpest knife, cutting deep into our innermost thoughts and desires. It exposes us for what we really are" (Hebrews 4:12, NLT).

And this is what we are really after—to become who we really are. To be brave, to silence the mysterious noise inside our soul that tells us we are alone. And the one place where strength for this journey can be found is in the "living power." You will find it on one side of the page in this book. On the other side is a survival note, inspiration to help you on this journey. For life can feel like a deserted island sometimes. You'll wonder if anyone is anywhere around. But He is here, like the knife, the sharpest knife, cutting through our darkness with holy light. Calming our fears. Keeping us safe. So relax. You will probably never be deserted on an island in the Pacific Ocean because God has other plans for your life.

*"For I know the plans I have for you," says the Lord.
"They are plans for good and not for disaster,
to give you a future and a hope."*

— Jeremiah 29:11, NLT

It is pleasant to see dreams come true . . .

~ ☼ ~

— Proverbs 13:19, NLT

ONE

HOW TO FOLLOW YOUR DREAMS

Dreams begin with anticipation. Life is built on hope. We hope to have a date for the prom. We hope to have enough money for a dress or to rent a tux. Then we start hoping for bigger things. We hope to get married someday. We hope to have a great job. But hope must have action. Goals must be set. Dreams have to be planned. And the way Noah planned his happiness was by accepting God's dream. God's dream was to have an ark that would sail above the stormy waters of a flood. And Noah built the ark in the middle of the desert. The nearest body of water was over a hundred miles away. And Noah kept hammering his eye-teeth out, even when people laughed. His goal was to fulfill God's dream. And true happiness takes place when we say, "God, here's my life. Give me your dreams." You do this and you will save yourself from drowning in an aimless sea.

Naming what you truly want means that you can begin to guide your life like a ship toward the harbor light, because you now have a goal that is exactly, precisely, and specifically identified.

— *Dr. Phil McGraw*

Love is patient, love is kind. It does not envy, it does not boast, it is not proud. It is not rude, it is not self-seeking, it is not easily angered, it keeps no record of wrongs. Love does not delight in evil but rejoices with the truth. It always protects, always trusts, always hopes, always perseveres.

— *1 Corinthians 13:4-7, NIV*

TWO
LOVE HURTS

Why does love hurt so badly sometimes? It hurts because we confuse love with self-respect. When someone breaks up with us, we feel rejection. And breakups are only painful when we focus on what has been taken away. And usually it is something that we have been getting from this person, such as attention or popularity. And what we mourn is really the absence of these things, not lost love.

You will know when you truly fall in love. You will become selfless. You will be more concerned with giving love, than receiving. You will give of your joy, of your understanding, of what it means to be alive. You will give rather than take. You will discover true love one day, just not yet. And when you do, it will never leave you. It will always protect. It will rejoice in the truth. It will always persevere if you let it.

> Nobody has ever measured, not even poets,
> how much the heart can hold.
> — *Zelda Fitzgerald*

Obviously, I'm not trying to be a people pleaser! No, I am trying to please God. If I were still trying to please people, I would not be Christ's servant.

~ ~

— *Galatians 1:10, NLT*

THREE

POPULARITY—WHO CAN AFFORD IT?

P opularity is the false belief that you have been chosen. Now you are safe from being seen as a loser. But what is popularity, anyway? Being in the right crowd? Wearing the in-clothes? Being more daring than the rest? Don't fall for this shallowness. Popularity contests are not truth contests. Ask the Apostle Peter. He tried to turn every encounter with Christ into a competition. He cut off a man's ear. He stepped out of the boat onto the shifting sea. He walked to Jesus only to sink. He wanted to show Christ that he was more willing, more daring than the rest. But anytime you walk on water to impress the crowd it does not last. You sink. You do not discover the acceptance you so desire.

So try to be honest with yourself and God.

> Fame is vapor, popularity an accident, riches take wings.
> Only one thing endures and that is character.
> — *Horace Greely*

There is a time for everything, and a
season for every activity under heaven . . .

— *Ecclesiastes 3:1, NIV*

FOUR

LET YOUR PARENTS GET SOME BEAUTY REST

Time is a taskmaster. Every second, minute, hour, and day are a whip at your back, churning out the decades. So stay up with time. Don't become its victim. Keep your curfews, and your curfews will keep you out of trouble. And time management is the key.

You only have so much time in each day and very little to waste. And the way you manage time wisely speaks volumes to your parents. They notice. Believe me they do. And when you excel in time management, they will not seem so controlling. And, remember, they are not trying to control you as much as they are your time. It might not seem like it, but there is a huge difference.

So think of curfews in measurements of time, not as a tool to control you. Plus, your parents are old. They need all the beauty rest they can get. So go easy on them. Get home on time, so they can get some sleep.

Time is what we want most, but . . . what we use worst.
— *Willam Penn*

The unfailing love of the Lord never ends! By his mercies we have been kept from complete destruction. Great is his faithfulness; his mercies begin afresh each day.

— *Lamentations 3:22-23, NLT*

FIVE

What Every New Day Brings

Every day is new in its own way. And in some ways, it remains the same. The sun rises in the east and sets in the west. But clouds can vary like the wind. They keep the weatherman guessing, "The forecast today will be partly cloudy." Tomorrow he may change it to rain. Every day has its voice. It speaks of something, like a birthday or the Fourth of July.

Days are new every morning and so are God's mercies. He works through the night like a cobbler in his shop, beating out the sin of us and fashioning the mercy He will bring. He stands at the door of every new day and knocks. And to open our days to Him is to get a fresh start. We put yesterday behind us. We lay down our grudges and our rebellion. We empty our hands. For new mercies He brings from the work of the cross. So let us begin each day here. We will find grace and mercy to help us in our time of need (Hebrews 4:16).

> If the end of one mercy were not
> the beginning of another, we were undone.
> — *Philip Henry*

For all have sinned; all fall
short of God's glorious standard.

— *Romans 3:23, NLT*

SIX

SWITCH PLACES WITH ONE PERSON IN YOUR SCHOOL

Life is merely a matter of trading. We trade earth for heaven, doubt for faith, guilt for forgiveness, if for when, instability for stability, fear for trust. These are accepted swaps. But what if you could become one person in your school for a day? Who would it be? And why? Do you know this person on the inside? Do you know what they weep for and laugh at the loudest?

Trading places with someone does not make our life different. We may discover that the person is beautiful, but feels ugly inside. They may have money and despise the father who makes it. They hurt just like us. Everyone is fighting the same battle—the battle against sin. It's at the root of every life. No one is without it. So stay where you are. Keep fighting the good fight of faith. Finish the race. Remain faithful (2 Timothy 4:7, NIV).

> You are totally unique, just like everyone else.
> — *Unknown*

Even perfection has its limits,
but your commands have no limit.

— Psalm 119:96, NLT

SEVEN

How to Alleviate Frustration

Frustration is the result of not feeling perfect. But some people cannot accept anything less. They want to be perfect in dress, perfect in looks, perfect in sports, and perfect academically. But even perfection has its limits. And those who believe they can attain perfection overextend themselves. They stretch their life thin, and frustration results. They are highly irritable. They have a temper and no tolerance for those who seem weak. But weak is where you want to be.

If your frustration level has peaked, it's a good sign that you are relying on your own strength. Alleviate frustration by acknowledging that you are human. Realize your limitations. Then trade your limitations for God's strength. "Look to the Lord and his strength; seek his face always" (Psalm 105:4). God doesn't ask us to be perfect, He only asks us to be dependent on His strength.

All that one needs in the battle of life is God's strength.
— *J.H. Jowett*

H ow painful are honest words!
But what do your arguments prove?

— *Job 6:25, NIV*

EIGHT

WALK AWAY FROM AN ARGUMENT

Arguing is the mind trying to be heard, not the heart. And it gets you nowhere. It only keeps raw emotions alive. And arguments only sour relationships. Unkind remarks can hurt our feelings. But you cannot even the score with your own hateful words. It never works. It only keeps things stirred up.

Each time you add a word to an already heated debate, you give it life. You keep the wound open. And usually there is a kernel of truth in every argument. You both are staking a claim in some truth. "How painful are honest words!" What is the truth of the argument? Why is it worth arguing over? Answering these questions can lead you to a new friendship. Evidently, you see some worth in this person or you wouldn't be emotionally involved. Sometimes arguments are really the beginning of great friendships. The way to find out is to let them have the last word. But before you do, find some common ground. Agree with them about one thing. You will be surprised at what happens next. Try it.

It takes two to quarrel, but only one to end it.
— *Spanish Proverb*

We are about to bring
a terrible disaster on ourselves!

— *Jeremiah 26:19, NIV*

NINE
NIP SIN IN THE BUD

We can get ourselves in trouble. And when we do, we like to blame others or our circumstances. "It was their idea, not mine." or "I had no choice in the matter." But the reality is no one holds a gun to our head. We willingly cheat. We purposely lie. We defy our curfew. So we cannot lay the blame on someone else. We make the decision to sin.

When our sins find us out, as they always do, we should be honest about our involvement. This way we cut the risk of bringing even more disaster our way. When we continue to lie and cover-up, we turn minimal punishment into disastrous punishment. And the people in Jeremiah's day were wise to understand the consequences of further unconfessed sin. So they nipped it in the bud. So should we.

> Forgive yourself for your faults
> and your mistakes and move on.
> — Les Brown

Jesus answered her, "If you knew the gift of God
and who it is that asks you for a drink,
you would have asked him and
he would have given you living water."

— *John 4:10, NIV*

TEN

HOW TO QUENCH YOUR THIRST

The world is a dusty, parched place. Sometimes it seems hard to find living water. Even when we cannot sense, or touch, or feel God touch us back, living water is still there. It is always there, flowing from the Throne of God to our doorstep. And if there is one mistake we all make, then it's running off in all directions before we drink of the living water. Because, when we drink, it flushes out all of the dusty, dead spots in our souls. It topples and washes away our mound of problems. It affirms that the world is a well-ordered and reliable place because God was before the world and He will be after it. So make sure you take a drink today. All you have to do is ask for it. "If you believe in me, come and drink! For the Scriptures declare that rivers of living water will flow out from within" (John 7:38, NLT). Inside is a geyser of living water. Take a drink. Let it flow.

> Trouble and perplexity drive us to prayer,
> and prayer driveth away trouble and perplexity.
> — *Philipp Melanchthon*

Hegai was very impressed with Esther and treated her kindly. He quickly ordered a special menu for her and provided her with beauty treatments.

— Esther 2:9, NLT

ELEVEN
GOT 2 BE BEAUTIFUL

Beauty has a lot to do with the beholder. But magazines will make you think you have to be beautiful to be loved. You should see some of the models without make-up, not a pretty sight. For even Esther needed some beauty treatment.

So when you see these models, imagine them on Monday morning. They don't crawl out of bed with mint breath and glossed lips. Everyone is human, which is why we all own a toothbrush and hygiene products. It is why we all need some beauty treatment. And what makes us attractive is self-assurance. Confidence covers a multitude of defects. Being comfortable in your own skin is more attractive than wanting to be someone else. Guys know when you are self-afflicted. They see how you treat yourself. And if you don't value yourself, don't expect them to either.

> All kinds of beauty do not inspire love;
> there is a kind which only pleases the sight,
> but does not captivate the affections.
> — *Cervantes*

They are wandering stars,
heading for everlasting gloom and darkness.

— *Jude 1:13, NLT*

TWELVE

WHERE STARS GO WHEN THEY DRIFT

Life is not a sure thing. We do not know what tomorrow brings. Things can happen. Accidents can occur. And this is the reason we should believe in God. For even lost stars become black holes. They drift into darkness when they lose their light. And no one really knows why. Some things are unknown. And what scares us about this verse is the mystery of it. Is life random? Where did the universe come from? These are questions that have stumped intelligent men and women. Theories abound. And whatever you accept as truth, know that God is the Creator. He hung the stars in the blackness. And the moment you begin to look to the source of light, instead of why this world is filled with darkness, is the instant that faith comes in. But the moment we doubt, we begin to drift away. And we know where things that drift go. They become black holes. They lose their purpose for being. They lose their radiance.

> What are ye orbs? The words of God?
> The Scriptures of the skies?
> — *Philip James Bailey*

F or I know the plans I have for you," says the Lord.
"They are plans for good and not for disaster,
to give you a future and a hope."

— *Jeremiah 29:11, NLT*

THIRTEEN
What's with All the Drama?

You will have bad days. They will litter the landscape of your life. Sometimes it feels like the world is against you. But don't go into doomsday hysterics. Your life is not ruined because of one lousy event. You can overcome it. But you cannot escape reality.

Running from ourselves is not possible. Everywhere we run, self will be right there. So forget about running. Remember, things we worry about seldom happen. We always find another date. We always get to play in another game. Our grades can be improved with hard work. But worrying does not help matters. So calm down. The day will always begin again. Afresh. Anew. Brimming with possibility. So ask yourself if this will matter in ten years.

Probably not.

> Do not measure your loss by itself; if you do, it will seem intolerable; but if you will take all human affairs into account you will find that some comfort is to be derived from them.
>
> — *St. Basil*

Do not lose heart or be afraid
when rumors are heard in the land;
one rumor comes this year,
another the next . . .

—— *Jeremiah 51:46, NIV*

FOURTEEN
How to Silence Nasty Rumors

Rumors have their cycles. You put a stop to one, another starts up. And maybe someone has been circulating false rumors about you. Know this, sometimes you can't defend yourself. I know what you're thinking: *I'll set them straight.* But usually it only makes things worse. So let a rumor run its course. It will die.

The source of a rumor is usually hard to find. "He said, she said" is the way rumors take on life. Don't worry about who said it. Calmly say it's not true. Then show them the real you. This is how you silence nasty rumors. You prove them wrong by your character. Composure is the secret, so stay calm, knowing that "one rumor comes this year, another the next . . ." There will always be rumors. Silence them by living a life that pleases God. "When the ways of people please the Lord, he makes even their enemies live at peace with them" (Proverbs 16:7, NLT).

> I cannot tell how the truth may be;
> I say the tale as 'twas said to me.
> — *Sir Walter Scott*

He who has been stealing must steal no longer, but must work, doing something useful with his own hands, that he may have something to share with those in need.

— *Ephesians 4:28, NIV*

FIFTEEN
What You Don't Have to Tell Winona Ryder

Shoplifting is a shame. Just ask Winona Ryder. No one looks good holding a board with numbers. Not even a movie star. So it's a shame that we do it thinking we won't get caught. "It will never happen to me." Yeah, right. It will. They will catch you on their candid camera. Some guy watches the monitor, eating cheese puffs. He's licking his fingers, one at a time, just waiting to bust you. Then he'll handcuff you, thumbprint you, and set off a flash in your face. You are recorded history. Your reputation is ruined. You will appear in court. And over what? A shirt? A pair of earrings? A trucker's hat?

Shoplifting really is stupid—but I don't have to tell Winona Ryder that.

> A thief believes everybody steals.
> — *Edward W. Howe*

The earth opened up and swallowed the men, along with their households and the followers who were standing with them, and everything they owned.

— *Numbers 16:32, NLT*

SIXTEEN

WHY THE EARTH MAY SWALLOW YOU

Moses was a patient soul. He put up with more people complaining in a day, than we will in a lifetime. They complained about not having water and about the food. And it's easy to become a complainer. "The food is lousy . . . I hate my teacher . . . I can't stand this place . . . My parents won't stop asking me questions . . . I wish they'd shut up." Complaining is a trap that is easy to fall into and hard to get out of. It's a habit. Try to catch yourself. Put a mark on your hand every time you complain. Count the marks at the end of the day. If you have over fifty, the ground may open up and swallow you. It happened to the Children of Israel!

> Avoid destructive thinking. Improper negative thoughts sink people. A ship can sail around the world many, many times, but just let enough water get into the ship and it will sink. Just so with the human mind. Let enough negative thoughts or improper thoughts get into the human mind and the person sinks just like a ship.
>
> — *Alfred A. Montapert*

But he was pierced for our transgressions, he was crushed for our iniquities; the punishment that brought us peace was upon him, and by his wounds we are healed.

— *Isaiah 53:5, NIV*

SEVENTEEN
THE PASSION OF CHRIST

they hung him
trees are tough
rings of sin that
displayed behind Him, what?

why a tree? why
not lions?
their mouths sharp with Pilate's
hands inside the bowl
of a helpless battle
draining into the Garden of
    Gethsemane

why a tree? why not
a shipwreck?
the coast sharp with the rock
of sages belonging to

bits and pieces
that would-be

why a tree? why for
the human race?
the wood cracking
His wound upon ours,
and the blood perpetuating
the cure of pain, ripped
open the soil when they
took Him down, and
can it ever be the same
inside the newness of something
I know now as life?

There is no health of the soul,
no hope of eternal life, save in the cross.
— *Thomas A. Kempis*

*W*ere you the first person ever born?
Were you born before the hills were made?

— *Job 15:7, NLT*

EIGHTEEN

DO YOUR PARENTS REALLY KNOW MORE THAN YOU?

Your mother may have worn tube tops and hot pants. Your father may have been a goober and owned a Ford Pinto with no muffler. Maybe he worked at Sonic on roller skates. But does this really mean that your parents are out of touch with your world?

You can bet on one thing—they fought with their parents. The struggle over choice of clothes and the time of curfew is nothing new under the sun. And the reason your parents cannot see your perspective is because they realize their parents knew more than they thought. Now they are trying to keep you from making the mistake of not listening to your parents.

So the next time your culture collides with theirs, ask yourself this question: "Are my parents being ridiculous or cautious?" The way you answer this question will change your reaction. Rebellion only makes things worse. So try asking your parents this question: "What would your parents say to me?" Now you are on level ground. Go from here. And be ready to listen.

We never know the love of our parents for us
until we have become parents.
— Henry Ward Beecher

So the Lord rescued Israel that day,
and the battle moved on beyond Beth Aven.

~ ☼ ~

— *1 Samuel 14:23, NIV*

NINETEEN

IS IT WORTH FIGHTING ABOUT?

Flies rested on the faces of the dead. Blood no longer gurgled in mortal wounds. The clash of Titans had moved on to Beth Aven. And there will be battles in your life. You will want to scream at someone. And usually it is someone who talks bad about you. But if you bite back, you give your critics what they want. They want pity. They want everyone to turn against you. They will tell everyone how badly you treated them, how you lied about them.

Some fights are not worth our time, neither are some people. So let the turmoil die. All you have to do is give it permission. You do this by remaining quiet. You do this by reminding yourself that all turmoil belongs to the devil. And the devil loves to sidetrack us with worthless drama. So put every fight to this question: "Is this meaningless?" If yes, keep your comments to yourself. Let the battle move on to Beth Aven.

Hating people is like burning down
your own house to get rid of a rat.
— *Harry Emerson Fosdick*

John replied, "God in heaven appoints each person's work."

— John 3:27, NLT

TWENTY

How to Discover Why You Are Here

"Why am I here?" is a daunting question. The simple answer is "You are here for a purpose." But trying to discover it can be frustrating.

The way to discover your destiny is to work while seeking God's presence. Do you feel close to God when you play sports or the piano? Do you feel close to God when you write in your journal or when you organize your school's student government?

The way to discover your destiny is to explore different roles. Sing in the church choir. Then ask, "Do I like being a team player?" Help an underprivileged kid with homework. Then ask, "Do I like working with people one-on-one?" Organize a fundraiser. Then ask, "Do I like to organize teams?"

When a task makes you feel close to God, this is your God-given ability. Now look for the occupations that are associated with your talents. Then you will discover why you are here. This is what living a purpose-filled life means.

Destiny is no matter of chance. It is a matter of choice.
It is not a thing to be waited for, it is a thing to be achieved.
— *William Jennings Bryan*

Then Pharaoh summoned Moses and Aaron and begged, "Plead with the Lord to take the frogs away from me and my people. I will let the people go, so they can offer sacrifices to the Lord."

"You set the time!" Moses replied . . .

"Do it tomorrow," Pharaoh said.

— *Exodus 8:8-10, NLT*

TWENTY-ONE
ONE MORE NIGHT WITH THE FROGS

Pharaoh wanted one more night with the frogs. It was a bonehead move. And maybe he was too tired to cleanup the mess of them. Maybe it was better to deal with it in the morning. There seems to be no logic behind his choice. But we do the same. We sleep with the frogs one more night. We tell God we will get our lives straightened out tomorrow. But tomorrow never comes for us. We wake up in the "Land of Us" and decide frogs are not that bad.

What is your frog? What is the one thing you are going to stop doing, but never do? For some it is a bad relationship. You keep kissing the frog that never becomes prince charming, and now you feel used. Or maybe you are having a problem with some kind of addiction. Whatever your frog may be, let it go back to the pond from which it came.

You do not need to be loved,
not at the cost of yourself.
— Jo Coudert

But among you there must not be
even a hint of sexual immorality . . .

— *Ephesians 5:3 NIV*

TWENTY-TWO
How Far Is Too Far

How far is too far sexually? It is a question you can't ask your bus driver. David Letterman will never have a Top Ten list of things you can't do sexually to remain pure. But know that you can cross the line without going all the way. It can happen in the backseat of a Ford. It can take place in the front seat of a Chevy beneath the moon. It can happen in a dark room while R. Kelly sings "Feelin' On Yo Booty." And just because you don't have sex doesn't make everything else okay.

The answer to "How far is too far?" can be answered by asking another question: "What would you do with your significant other if Christ were in the room?" Now maybe that's taking things too far. Or is it?

Complete abstinence is easier than perfect moderation.
— *St. Augustine*

Then Saul gave David his own armor—a bronze helmet and a coat of mail. David put it on, strapped the sword over it, and took a step or two to see what it was like, for he had never worn such things before. "I can't go in these," he protested. "I'm not used to them." So he took them off again.

— *1 Samuel 17:38-39, NLT*

TWENTY-THREE
What to Do When Your Heart
Weighs a Ton of Bricks

It was the match of the century—a giant versus a skinny shepherd boy. And the odds on the street had Goliath winning by KO. And King Saul didn't want David to get creamed. So he made David wear his armor. But the helmet didn't fit. The sword hung on him like a bed rail. He walked like a man in oversize galoshes through a snowstorm. Each step a laborious muddling through the sand. So he took the armor off and loaded his slingshot.

The world tells us to fight our battles the world's ways. And this could include drugs and alcohol, which only intensifies the situation, instead of relieving it. So the way to win over guilt, worry, sadness, or despair is to fight like David. He knew he couldn't fight with a bed rail strapped to his side. So it is with our soul. A heart that weighs a ton of bricks needs a Savior with mighty strength, "so that your faith might not rest on men's wisdom, but on God's power" (1 Corinthians 2:5, NIV).

> The strength of a man consists in finding out
> the way God is going, and going in that way too.
> — *Henry Ward Beecher*

She will chase after her lovers
but not catch them.

— *Hosea 2:7, NIV*

TWENTY-FOUR
WHEN YOU WANT THE ONE YOU CAN'T HAVE

So you love the one you cannot have. Now you feel trapped like a goldfish in a plastic bag at a carnival. The world is one big slosh. One minute you feel one way about the person, then you feel different the next. You wake up thinking of them. You go to bed and dream about them. And it seems the more they ignore you the worse it gets.

Stop torturing yourself. Just because you are being rejected doesn't mean you are cursed for life. It may just mean this person is wrong for you. And the right one will come along. God will bring that special someone into your life. So don't get down on yourself. Your prince charming is on his way. Your princess is only trapped in the tower for now. You will rescue her. And you will live happily ever after, as much as one can in this fallen world.

> To love someone who does not love you, is like
> shaking a tree to make the dew drops fall.
> — *Unknown Proverb*

All who hate me whisper about me,
imagining the worst for me.

— *Psalm 41:7, NLT*

TWENTY-FIVE
How to Find Out If You Are Hated By Your Friends

It is hard to know who hates you, who *really* hates you. No one will tell you to your face. It usually happens behind your back. So how does someone find out who hates them? Before I give you the answer, jot down in 30 seconds the initials of those you dislike. Ready. Go.

The reason I asked you to do this is because it was once an experiment. Psychologists asked a group of college students to jot down in 30 seconds the initials of people they disliked. Some could only think of one person, some listed as many as 14. This is what they discovered: Those who disliked the largest number, were themselves the most disliked.

Was your list long?

> I shall never permit myself to stoop
> so low as to hate any man.
> — *Booker T. Washington*

Godly sorrow brings repentance that leads to salvation and leaves no regret, but worldly sorrow brings death.

— *2 Corinthians 7:10, NIV*

TWENTY-SIX
WHERE GOD TIES A YELLOW RIBBON

Guilt is not godly sorrow. Guilt is a turn from God that offers no way back. It condemns us and makes us feel broken. It is sorrow without hope. But godly sorrow is the remorse we feel when we hurt someone we love. Now we want the hurt to subside. Now we want Him as much as He does us. Because godly sorrow is what we feel when God ties a yellow ribbon around our soul. We understand He wants us to come home.

Godly sorrow is the joy of return. It is one giant step away from sin. It is one small step toward the Savior. And we take down the yellow ribbon and replace it with a crimson one. That forever reminds us that it is by His blood we are saved. Because He is the lover of our soul. And to sin is to hurt Him. And we can never do that without feeling godly sorrow. But who wants to feel that?

> The knowledge of sin is the beginning of salvation.
> — *Epicurus*

And I want women to be modest in their appearance. They should wear decent and appropriate clothing and not draw attention to themselves by the way they fix their hair or by wearing gold or pearls or expensive clothes.

— *1 Timothy 2:9, NLT*

TWENTY-SEVEN
THE COW COVERING YOUR BODY

Leather was once for bikers. Now it looks good on rock stars. It fits snug on movie stars too. But certain church members may not like the cow covering your body. *So what is the godly way to dress? Can I show cleavage? Can I expose my midriff? Can my pants sag below my back?*

The Bible does not outline a strict dress code. It does not say leather is in and spandex is out. It says there should be modesty. And modesty always brings beauty to mind, instead of sexual tension. So be aware of how your clothing can beg for lust. But also know that lust can happen regardless. Even if we clad ourselves from head-to-toe in armor, lust will find an expression. So you cannot stop lust. It is evil. And it always interprets God's creation in twisted ways. But you can curb it by being modest.

Modesty has to do with our intentions—a matter of the heart. And when you dress seductively to get attention, you have crossed the line.

One of the most attractive things about the flowers
is their beautiful reserve.
— *Henry David Thoreau*

Beginning a quarrel is like opening a floodgate,
so drop the matter before a dispute breaks out.

— *Proverbs 17:14, NLT*

TWENTY-EIGHT

3 STEPS TO WORKING THINGS OUT IN A RELATIONSHIP

1. *Be willing to sit down and discuss things.*
   Relationships are two-way streets. You must desire to be together. Staying in a relationship just because you don't want to hurt someone's feelings only makes it worse. If you love them, work it out. If not, move on. You will both feel better.

2. *Be honest.*
   You may be fighting because you are unable to tell them the truth about something that gets on your nerves. So tell them. Just do it in love. Don't blast them. But get it all out.

3. *Be Forgiving.*
   Let the past be the past. Don't write a history book. No one likes it when the past is thrown up in their face. Forgive and try to forget. Then make a new start.

> The ultimate test of a relationship
> is to disagree, but to hold hands.
> — *Alexandra Penney*

The wise are glad to be instructed,
but babbling fools fall flat on their faces.

— *Proverbs 10:8, NLT*

TWENTY-NINE
NOBODY SHOVED HUMPTY DUMPTY

Did Humpty Dumpty jump or was he pushed? Conspiracy theories abound. Maybe someone dared him. "Humpty Dumpty, I dare you to jump." And he accepted. He dared to jump and climb the wall again. But he fell flat on his face. He shattered. And for what?

Dares make us feel special. This is why we accept them. We want attention and recognition. So we cheat. We lie. We jump off bridges. We drag race. But we never think beyond the dare. We just do it. And things can happen when we accept dares. We can break a leg, wreck a car, hurt someone else, or get in trouble with the police.

Remember, if you feel like Superman, you may need to check your cape. It may be cutting off circulation to your brain. And this can make an empty head come unglued. And when you jump, it won't be pretty.

> Nothing in the world is more dangerous than
> sincere ignorance and conscientious stupidity.
> — *Martin Luther King, Jr.*

Still, when I tried to figure it out,
all I got was a splitting headache . . .

— *Psalm 73:16, NIV*

THIRTY
WHEN YOUR PARENTS DIVORCE

Maybe your parents have divorced. Now you feel like your whole life has been one big lie. This is normal. All of us question life when it seemingly falls apart. But the dream of a happy family has not died. It still lurks in the cavity of pain. Your father is still your father; your mother is still your mother. This has not changed. What has changed is the way you view your family. Everything has become jagged parts. Divorce splits reality. But life can become complete again. The pain will heal.

The first step toward healing is to accept what has happened. In most cases, divorce is final. You probably will not get your parents back together. So don't turn your hurt into anger toward them. It only makes things worse. And remember, your life is not a lie. Things have just changed. That's all. Try to see this as a new beginning. Let go of the pain.

Happiness is acceptance.
— *Anonymous*

The Lord said to my Lord,
"Sit in honor at my right hand until
I humble your enemies beneath your feet."

— *Mark 12:36, NLT*

THIRTY-ONE
BENEATH A BIG HAIRY TOE

What is beneath your feet at this moment? It could be every piece of clothing you have scattered across every inch of your bedroom. Or it could be freshly vacuumed carpet. Or it may be a waxed hardwood floor. Look down, what do you see? Big hairy toes or polished toe nails?

Did you know that biologists have discovered an average of 1,356 living creatures in the top inch of forest soil? Every square foot includes 865 mites, 265 spring tails, 22 millipedes, 19 adult beetles, and various numbers of 12 other forms. All of this right below our feet when we hike through the woods!

Beneath Jesus' feet is His enemy. The devil is His footstool. And so it is with those who walk with Christ. The devil is beneath our feet. And we only have to keep him from tripping us up. But when we walk with Christ, He points out the devil's schemes. So tread on. Put your big hairy toes on the devil's head. It will feel so good.

> Every evil in the bud is easily crushed;
> as it grows older, it becomes stronger.
> — *Cicero*

Don't use foul or abusive language. Let everything you say be good and helpful, so that your words will be an encouragement to those who hear them.

— Ephesians 4:29, NLT

THIRTY-TWO
How to Know If Evil Lurks in the Heart

No one likes a nasty mouth, even if it has a beautiful face. And foul language may be in every conversation you hear. It is in most music and movies, too. Society makes cussing seem so hip. But listen to cuss words. Most are putdowns. It is a language of cynicism. It mirrors what is inside a person.

Jesus said, "For whatever is in your heart determines what you say" (Matthew 12:34, NLT). This is how you can tell what is in someone's heart. If evil is there, they will speak it. They will complain. They will say hateful things to people. Because if there is one thing you cannot hide it is an evil heart. Your mouth will tell the world.

> Half the world is composed of people who have something to say and can't, and the other half who have nothing to say and keep on saying it.
>
> — *Robert Frost*

The water receded steadily from the earth. At the end of the hundred and fifty days the water had gone down, and on the seventeenth day of the seventh month the ark came to rest on the mountains of Ararat.

— *Genesis 8:3-4, NIV*

THIRTY-THREE
WHERE TO REST YOUR SOUL

The ark creaked like an old wooden floor. Every step was a reminder. If it was not for the storm outside, Noah could never have stood the stench inside. But there stood Noah on a forty day and forty night cruise. No certain destination. Just a longing for a shore. And what the old tub hit was probably the top of a mountain. It creaked and popped and jolted its passengers. It grinded to a halt. And the look on Noah's face said it all, "It will soon be over." And the dove brought a sprig of hope.

Maybe you need a sprig of hope. Something to heal your broken heart. Something to end the flood. Maybe you are longing for a shore, somewhere to rest your soul. There is a hill called Calvary, where sin comes to a grinding halt. And this is what we are really looking for, some place to cleanse our soul. Some place to run aground, to stop the madness of the float across a world that would just as soon drown us.

> God is not a power or principle or law, but he is a living, creating, communicating person—a mind who thinks, a heart who feels, a will who acts, whose best name is Father.
> — *Robert Hamill*

Silence is praise to you, Zion—
dwelling God, And also obedience.

— *Psalm 65:1, NIV*

Keep on praying.

— *1 Thessalonians 5:17, NLT*

THIRTY-FOUR
WHAT HAPPENS WHEN YOU KEEP YOUR MOUTH SHUT

Silence is a monk's outer garment. But we never think of silence as being worship. Try going through your day like a monk. Impossible? Maybe. Being quiet is like losing contact with the world. It is like living in a bubble. But you will find yourself closer to God. It will help you develop communication with Him. He is the only one who can speak without saying a word. The Apostle Paul believes we should "pray all the time." It is the act of conversing with God on a non-stop basis.

Go through your day with God present in your every thought. Treat Him like a friend. Include Him in every conversation. You will discover yourself staying away from gossip. You will be less competitive for attention.

> Prayer is the place of refuge for every worry, a foundation for cheerfulness, a source of constant happiness, a protection against sadness.
> — *St. John Chrysostom*

We do not dare to classify or compare ourselves with some who commend themselves. When they measure themselves by themselves and compare themselves with themselves, they are not wise.

— *2 Corinthians 10:12, NIV*

THIRTY-FIVE
NEVER COMPARE YOURSELF TO OTHERS

What would it be like to live next door to a perfect person? Their lawn would be perfect, their rooms ideal. And we would feel incomplete and broken. We would always be comparing ourselves with how we should be. But the sad thing is we do it anyway. We compare ourselves to those we think have it all together. And what if we stopped comparing ourselves to others? Would we be closer to happiness?

Instead of comparing yourself to others, what if you tried to discover what makes others successful? Take note of where they succeed. Watch how they fail. But never, ever compare yourself with them. It leads to two extreme opposites: 1) self-righteousness or 2) an inferiority-complex. Both extremes cripple us. They make it hard for us to love and be loved.

To him that watches, everything is revealed.
— *Italian Proverb*

So give your parents joy!

~ ☼ ~

— Proverbs 23:25, NLT

THIRTY-SIX

DISARMING YOUR PARENTS

Parents can get in your business. They want to know every move you make. They watch what you eat and try to look over your shoulder. "Do this . . . Do that . . . Where are you going?" That's all they seem to say. It makes you want to scream. But you're stuck with them. They are not going to run away to Tahiti. So do the best you can. This means disarm them. Weapon reduction is the key. Take away their worry by communicating the next move before they ask. This will set them back on their heels. Then go for the jugular. Cleanup your room. Put dishes in the dishwasher. The results will be on their face. This is the joy of it. But it also gets them off your back.

So stay one step ahead. Do the unexpected. ". . . live a life of steady goodness so that only good deeds will pour forth." This will silence any parent and show you are wise. And being wise gets you some breathing room.

> Youth is when you blame all your troubles on your parents . . .
> — *Harold Coffin*

A relaxed attitude lengthens life;
jealousy rots it away.

~ ☼ ~

— *Proverbs 14:30, NLT*

THIRTY-SEVEN
WHY YOU SHOULD NEVER DATE A JEALOUS PERSON

Jealousy is a cul-de-sac of insecurity. It goes around with no way out. It asks a thousand questions. "Where were you? . . . Who were you with?" Jealous people have counterfeit emotions that erupt into a head game of accusations. They just know you like someone else. They can feel it. They believe you have been ignoring them. And their accusations are always ridiculous.

Avoid jealous people. They will make your life miserable. Sure, it feels good in the beginning. Who doesn't like the attention of jealousy? But remember that jealousy is a mark of an unhealthy relationship. You will never be able to convince them of your devotion. So move on. Don't waste your time trying to please a jealous person. Once you try to prove them wrong, it only makes them more suspicious.

> Jealousy, that dragon which slays love
> under the pretense of keeping it alive.
> — *Havelock Ellis*

The disciples did not understand any of this. Its meaning was hidden from them, and they did not know what he was talking about.

— *Luke 18:34, NIV*

THIRTY-EIGHT
MESSAGE IN A BODY

You are like a bottle washed up on a deserted island. And inside a message longs to be read. But no one seems to care. You even say, "No one understands!" You say it over and over again.

There was a message inside of Christ. "Its meaning was hidden from them . . ." Hidden because they could not comprehend, hidden because they selfishly wanted Christ to be a conquering king over Rome's persecution. They made Christ into what they wanted Him to be. But the Lord is not our Genie-in-a-bottle. The only thing He grants is a hidden message in a bottle: "Come to Me, all of you who have washed up on the beach. Hold My Hand. See My Heart." And love is all He ever wanted from His disciples. And they finally got the message when the bottle was broken and He hung there on the Cross.

Now 2000 years later, the broken body is gone. But the Message remains: "Come to Me. See My Heart. I understand your pain."

Today, may our prayer be, "You have been my help; do not leave me nor forsake me, O God of my salvation. Amen."
— *Charles Haddon Spurgeon*

I tell you the truth, unless you change and become like little children, you will never enter the kingdom of heaven.

— *Matthew 18:3, NIV*

THIRTY-NINE
BECOMING A CHILD AGAIN

Little children are unpredictable. Who knows what they will say and do? They may throw a temper tantrum and say, defiantly, "No!" But they're also innocent. They like to play. They do not worry about the grass stain on their jeans. They do not worry about how they smell.

The child never leaves us. We just stretch in our skin. We develop. We shave. We talk on cell phones and worry about how to dress, about how to act to have friends. And we lose our innocence. We just live to meet the demands of the world. We forget to come aside and live as a child. Forget to let go of worrying about how we fit in. Forget to abandon ourselves to love, never thinking more highly of ourselves than we should. We become as a child when we crawl up into Jesus' lap in an instance. No thoughts of what wickedness He might see in us. Just a child ready to be loved by the King.

> We are most nearly ourselves when
> we achieve the seriousness of the child at play.
> — *Heraclitus*

If one falls down, his friend can help him up. But pity the man who falls and has no one to help him up!

— *Ecclesiastes 4:10, NIV*

FORTY
LIFE IS A TEAM SPORT

Life is a team sport. We need each other. But we will not get everybody's help. Each friend in our life adds strength to our character. Good friends are those who know everything about us and love us anyway. Friends never demand more than who we are. But they challenge us to become all that we can be. They look beyond who we are to what we may become. When Jesus called Simon Peter a rock, Simon Peter was everything but. He fled from Jesus' crucifixion. He lied about being his friend (Matthew 26:70). But in the end, he became the rock that Jesus predicted.

Always look for the best in people before you see the worst. A friend is one who never forsakes, no matter what the case. As friends we never become involved in other's recklessness. We're there to help them back up after a fall. There are only a small number of lifetime friends. And some will be the friends you are making now.

Little friends may prove great friends.
— *Aesop*

I am not ashamed of the gospel, because it is the power of God for the salvation of everyone who believes: first for the Jew, then for the Gentile.

— *Romans 1:16, NIV*

FORTY-ONE
TOOTHPASTE IS FOR TEETH, NOT ZITS

Most of us have tried to put toothpaste on a zit. But it doesn't cure acne. It may only dry the surface a little. There are some people whose holiness is only on the surface. It doesn't penetrate to the root of their character. The difference between *acting* holy and *being* holy can be recognized. Most people know how to read a soul. We watch your actions outside the spotlight of popularity. We listen when you talk in a small group. We hear you when you down others to make yourself look good. We know a fake when we watch one, because fake holiness is only skin-deep.

Let inner holiness determine outward behavior. Be the same person inside and out. Don't be ashamed of being a Christian. Be true to God first. "Don't just pretend that you love others. Really love them. Hate what is wrong. Stand on the side of the good" (Romans 12:9, NLT).

Hypocrite: Someone who complains that
there is too much sex and violence on his VCR.
— *Unknown*

Jesus said to them, "You belong to your father, the devil, and you want to carry out your father's desire. He was a murderer from the beginning, not holding to the truth, for there is no truth in him. When he lies, he speaks his native language, for he is a liar and the father of lies."

— *John 8:42-44, NIV*

FORTY-TWO

HOW TO CREATE YOUR OWN PRISON

Everyone hates being lied too. But some people secretly enjoy lying to others. It makes them feel powerful. They feel like they are creating something. And they are—their own demise. This is the danger of lying. It makes us one with Satan. It is his native tongue—the way he creates something from nothing. He builds his own world on a stack of lies. And his world will crumble one day. So stand back. Those who lie are in danger of going down with him. It is a prison.

No one can follow God's plan by building on the sinking sands of a lie. What will come through loud and clear will be Satan's plan for your life. This is the danger of lying. "You belong to your father, the devil, and you want to carry out your father's desire" (John 8:44, NIV).

> Sin has many tools, but
> a lie is the handle that fits them all.
> — *Oliver Wendell Holmes, Sr.*

. . . A time to weep and a time to laugh,
a time to mourn and a time to dance.

— Ecclesiastes 3:4, NIV

FORTY-THREE
WHAT TO SAY AT A FUNERAL

Mourning seems to be the most difficult part of life. In the Old Testament, mourners shaved their heads. They smeared ashes on their faces. It was a show of solidarity. But today, we put on suits and ties. Women wear black. And a hearse takes you away.

Funerals are always awkward. Where do you stand? What do you say? Things like that pop in your head when you enter a funeral parlor. Some of us say too much at funerals. Those who mourn do not need a biblical explanation. Leave this to the clergy. What they need is your presence. So be careful not to ruin it with words. This is why people shaved their heads and smeared ashes on their face. They wanted their actions to speak a lament better than words. So, at a funeral, simply say, "I'm praying for you." That is it. Nothing else. They will need your words later. Somewhere down the road.

Life is pleasant. Death is peaceful.
It's the transition that's troublesome.
— *Matthew Arnold*

Jacob found a stone for a pillow and lay down to sleep. As he slept, he dreamed of a stairway that reached from earth to heaven. And he saw the angels of God going up and down on it.

— *Genesis 28:11-12, NLT*

FORTY-FOUR
PLAY ETERNITY AGAINST REALITY

Lonely days will happen. Relationships will end. Parties will take place and you will not receive an invitation. And sometimes it can feel as though you are cursed by God. The world can be one lonely place. But just above your head, just beyond your sight, angels tread. So when you feel alone, take on an eternal view. Open your eyes to the invisible. Play eternity against reality. Scripture always points us in this direction. Its eyes are ever forward. So take on an eternal view by asking yourself if what you feel right now will be felt in heaven. Will it matter there?

Eternity is the true substance of life in the end. So try your best to let eternity stamp your moments with its reality.

> Faith is to believe what you do not see;
> the reward of this faith is to see what you believe.
> — *St. Augustine*

But many who seem to be important now will be the least important then, and those who are considered least here will be the greatest then.

— *Matthew 19:30, NIV*

FORTY-FIVE
New Way to Be Human

One thing to recognize in life. One thing to know. Life on this planet may be backwards. The least here will be the greatest in heaven. And what if the part of the Lord's Prayer, "Thy will be done on earth as it is in heaven,"(Matthew 6:10) is Jesus' way of preparing us for this switch? The guy with the bad complexion, the crooked teeth, hook-nose, and bifocals, may win a superlative in heaven. The sick could be the star athletes. The poor could be the rich. The janitor could be the most important faculty member. Think of it. It would mean a new way to be human.

So what if we turned our worlds upside down? Would we be nice to the poor? Would we vote for the not so attractive to win a superlative? Would we change the category to "Least likely to succeed?" It is worth our thoughts, because something is going to change. The first here is going to be last there. This much is true. So how does that change the way we live?

The unfortunate thing about this world is that the good habits are much easier to give up than the bad ones.
— William Somerset Maugham

Yes, I am the vine; you are the branches. Those who remain in me, and I in them, will produce much fruit. For apart from me you can do nothing.

— *John 15:5, NLT*

FORTY-SIX

EXPOSURE TO THE SON

Suntans are hard to keep. They glow and fade like a lightning bug. They feed off the sun and go white in darkness. The only way to keep a suntan is to stay in the sun's presence. In the presence of the sun the tan darkens and becomes a golden asset. People look good with a suntan, but suntans can be dangerous. And I'm not pushing suntans. But your relationship with God works much like a suntan. You have to keep yourself exposed to the Son. The moment you step out of the Lord's presence, your soul will be drawn to darkness. And the longer you remain in darkness, the more your soul is malnourished. Then we cry, "I don't feel the Lord's presence!"

If you want a tan, stay in the sun. If you want to be spiritual, stay close to the Son. This is why Jesus said, "For apart from me you can do nothing" (John 15:5, NLT).

> Being a Christian is more than just an instantaneous
> conversion; it is like a daily process whereby
> you grow to be more and more like Christ.
> — *Billy Graham*

As long as Moses held up his hands, the Israelites were winning, but whenever he lowered his hands, the Amalekites were winning. When Moses' hands grew tired, they took a stone and put it under him and he sat on it. Aaron and Hur held his hands up—one on one side, one on the other—so that his hands remained steady till sunset.

— *Exodus 17:11-12, NIV*

FORTY-SEVEN
WHAT WE WORRY ABOUT

Moses won the battle hands up, not down. Each time his strength gave way and his elbows lowered, the Amalekites would begin to win. But when he kept them raised, Israel would win. And who knows why the victory resided in Moses' outstretched arms? Perhaps, it was an act of prayer. And what a wonderful picture of prayer—hands up in submission to God. This is how prayer fills us. It comes through submission to God.

Try this: write out your prayers in a journal. Keep them short. Then beside each prayer write the things you fear may happen. Try it for two weeks. Then go back. See if God answered your prayers. Then check to see how many of the things you worried about really happened. 90% of the things we worry about never occur.

> The sovereign cure for worry is prayer.
> — *William James*

When they saw the courage of Peter and John and realized that they were unschooled, ordinary men, they were astonished and they took note that these men had been with Jesus.

— *Acts 4:13, NIV*

FORTY-EIGHT
How to Become Great

"What did I do to deserve this?" You will ask yourself this question. Everyone does at some point in the journey. People get mad at us for no reason. Others blame us for something we didn't do. And when you ask yourself this question, you are victimizing yourself. You are saying, "I'm helpless. I'm a victim of circumstance." But do not make yourself the victim. It will cause you to become what other people say you are. The world will always try to label you. But remember that identity is yours to make. You control what you become. And when labeled, prove the label wrong. Be yourself. Let Christ shape your identity. This is what Peter and John did. They were ordinary men who became great by spending time with Jesus.

> Should envious tongues some malice frame;
> to soil and tarnish your good name;
> Live it Down!
> — *Henry Rink*

Now Abel kept flocks, and Cain worked the soil. In the course of time Cain brought some of the fruits of the soil as an offering to the Lord. But Abel brought fat portions from some of the firstborn of his flock. The Lord looked with favor on Abel and his offering, but on Cain and his offering he did not look with favor. So Cain was very angry, and his face was downcast.

— *Genesis 4:1-5, NIV*

FORTY-NINE
I HATE MY BROTHER!

Abel carried a slingshot. And Cain dressed in overalls. Abel could count sheep and never get sleepy. But Cain could not stand the smell of them. The only place he wanted to be was behind a plow. And these two brothers were entirely different from one another. God had uniquely wired each. And Cain felt that he was being played as the lesser brother, especially after his sacrifice was rejected.

And maybe you feel like you are being compared to a sibling. Maybe you feel the pressure of their legacy. Maybe they were the high school star athlete. Maybe they won homecoming queen. This can mean a lot of pressure. So tell your parents how you feel. And know that it is not like this with God. Everybody comes to God on a level playing field. But Cain approached God on his own terms. A big mistake! He believed a sacrifice was too bloody, too demeaning. And God rejected it. And Cain raised hell and killed his brother. Then he had to live with the guilt of it.

> You cannot make yourself feel something you do not feel,
> but you can make yourself do right in spite of your feelings.
> — *Pearl Buck, Author of* The Good Earth

He reveals the deep things of darkness and
brings deep shadows into the light.

— Job 12:22, NIV

FIFTY

STEPPING OUT OF THE SHADOWS OF AN EATING DISORDER

We can be too thin and never know it. It is the trick of the mirror. But really, it is inside our mind. And somewhere deep inside we know this. We have buried the sane voice that begs us to stop. We have silenced it and convinced ourselves otherwise. Sure, everyone wants to look good. This is not a problem. But when being too thin affects our health, we don't look so good. We actually look worse.

Being honest with ourselves is how we bring dark secrets into the light. And this is the hardest part about an eating disorder. We have to admit we have a problem. We have to realize we are powerless against it without help. And to bring this into the light doesn't mean we are a bad person. It means we are moving toward being healthy again. And this is a good thing.

If you are having a problem with an eating disorder, please talk to someone. You will feel so much better.

> One of the secrets of life is to make
> stepping stones out of stumbling blocks.
> — *Jack Penn*

*W*as it for nothing that I kept my heart pure
and kept myself from doing wrong?

—— *Psalm 73:13, NLT*

FIFTY-ONE
THE ODDS OF GETTING CAUGHT CHEATING

Cheaters win—sometimes. They seem so sly and good at it. And you will be tempted to cheat. It is a natural impulse. You may even get away with it once or twice. Cheating is like playing Russian roulette. The bullet will eventually engage and fire. And you will pay the price. Cheaters always have to pay for their deception. Don't be fooled by their immediate success, because in the end, they pay by having no education. They pay with the evil contour of their soul. And this is too high a price for a good grade in some class. Plus, cheaters always get caught—if not in this world, then in the one to come. So don't get focused on cheating the way the psalmist did. He felt stupid for playing by the rules. But being honest is what will matter in the end. "Wealth created by lying is a vanishing mist and a deadly trap" (Proverbs 21:6, NLT).

> An honorable man or woman is one who is truthful; free from deceit; above cheating, lying, stealing, or any form of deception. An honorable man or woman is one who learns early that one cannot do wrong and feel right.
>
> — *Ezra Taft Benson*

Everything that is now hidden or secret
will eventually be brought to light.

— *Mark 4:22, NLT*

FIFTY-TWO

WHAT YOU DO IN SECRET WILL BE
SHOUTED IN THE HALLS

Some boys love to brag. They can be heard all over the school. They sweet talk and hunt down their victims. Then they ruin a girl's reputation. So don't think what is done under the guise of love and secrecy will not be heard. Boys like to talk about their escapades. They love taking trophies. Grant it, some girls don't care. Some girls brag as much as the guys. But if your innocence is stolen and put out on display, it will kill you inside. You will feel as if you have been used and hung up as a trophy for all to see. And you will become the target of gossip. When we get used, it never sounds good whispered from ear-to-ear. Guard your innocence. Keep it to yourself, and it will keep you from the kind of gossip that rattles and hums down through the long halls.

> I usually get my stuff from people who promised
> somebody else that they would keep it a secret.
> — *Walter Winchell*

From the sixth hour until the ninth hour darkness came over all the land. About the ninth hour Jesus cried out in a loud voice, "Eloi, Eloi, lama sabachthani?" —which means, "My God, my God, why have you forsaken me?"

— *Matthew 27:45-46, NIV*

FIFTY-THREE
THE SILENCE OF GOD

Silence is holy work. It allows us to do some thinking. And out of these thoughts in solitude, we can discover the next step. So may the world go away and leave us in silence with the Lord. So we can listen. So He can speak. And when He chooses not to speak, He has a reason. Because it is in silence that He does His best work.

Behind the sixth hour until the ninth, God's silence was a redeeming force. When Christ cried out, God answered with silence. Not a word. It had to be that way. Because when God seems silent, He is working behind our dark clouds, redeeming our problems. So let us wait in silence, as before His throne. "But the Lord is in his holy temple: let all the earth keep silence before him" (Habakkuk 2:20, NIV). For in His holy temple sits the desk of His great work. And spread before Him are your problems and mine. And in the silence, divine intervention works.

> We need to find God, and he cannot be found in noise and restlessness. God is the friend of silence. See how nature—trees, flowers, grass—grows in silence; see the stars, the moon and the sun, how they move in silence.
> — *Mother Teresa*

"Simon, Simon, Satan has asked to have all of you, to sift you like wheat. But I have pleaded in prayer for you, Simon, that your faith should not fail. So when you have repented and turned to me again, strengthen and build up your brothers."

Peter said, "Lord, I am ready to go to prison with you, and even to die with you."

— Luke 22:31-33, NLT

FIFTY-FOUR
What to Do When You Fall

Peter's mouth was larger than his faith. And Satan cleaned his clock. He rammed Peter's words back down his raspy throat. And Peter choked. He stumbled. He spat out denial.

If only he would have listened. But he was to busy talking and waving his ego. He was ready to get a mug shot taken if he had to. He would go to prison. He would even die if it came to that. But Peter did not act on his words. They were hollow. And most of us say we will do more than we ever accomplish. And the great thing about this tragedy is Jesus' grace. "So when you have repented and turned to me again . . ."

This was probably something Peter did not hear at the time. But, later, Jesus' words must have brought him comfort. Christ still believed in him. He was not too far gone. And neither are you. Turn to Him. Accept the grace that has been available before you even fell. Then make a change.

> The most powerful idea that's entered the world in the last few thousand years—the idea of grace—is the reason I would like to be a Christian.
>
> — *Bono, U2*

My thoughts grew hot within me and began to burn, igniting a fire of words.

~ ☼ ~

— *Ephesians 4:31, NLT*

FIFTY-FIVE
ANGER MANAGEMENT

Anger can get out of hand. It can make us say things we might regret. Thoughts can grow hot within us and begin to burn. And this is when things get ugly, igniting a fire of words. The seams of our sanity come undone. Then we shout and stomp and hit and argue. We may never intentionally do this. Usually, we are not impulsive and hard to get along with. But there are people who know how to push our buttons. They have studied the very fibers of our personality. They know just the right spot. And they can push, but we don't have to react. We can take away the button and control our emotions. This makes us an observer of anger and not a participant.

He who angers you conquers you.
— *Elizabeth Kenny*

So don't be dismayed when the wicked grow rich,
and their homes become ever more splendid.

— *Psalm 49:16, NLT*

FIFTY-SIX
Watch Me Pull a Woman Out of My Hat!

The tricks of MTV are impressive to watch. They make it look so good. The flash and the movements, even the beat can get inside your head. Then there are the women, lots of women. They litter the landscape. They hang on the musicians like the gold around their necks. They pierce the screen like body jewelry. But don't be fooled by the tattoo of fame. It is short-lived. And their riches? They usually wind up squandering it all. Money will never create the lifestyle portrayed in music videos.

Happiness is not a Rolls-Royce and ten girls at your feet. Women are not toys. They are to be esteemed and honored. Making them gyrate for your pleasure is degrading. Women are not stage props for music videos. If you treat a woman like most women are treated in music videos, you will find loneliness. Never fall for the trick of MTV. It is not real life. Women want respect.

> Men are respectable only as they respect.
> — *Ralph Waldo Emerson*

. . . *A* companion of fools suffers harm.

~ ☼ ~

— *Proverbs 13:20, NIV*

FIFTY-SEVEN
JOYRIDES CAN END IN DISASTER

Cars are what we want, especially at sixteen. We want to grip the steering wheel and hit the open highway in the great American night. Cars are our own private space, a voyage below the stars. This is the joy of the ride. It is freedom. But it also brings responsibility. So watch out for the person who is not watching out for you. Other motorists don't always have your best interest at heart. They are in their own cocoon, just like you. But metal crashing into metal is the collision of two separate worlds. Never fall for the feeling of safety that a car seemingly provides. Remember you are "a companion of fools" when sharing the open road. Some are drunk. Some are talking on their cell phones. Some are simply not paying attention. They can be erratic, off their side of the road and into your private space without warning. So be aware at all times and enjoy the ride.

It is better to be safe than sorry.
— *American Proverb*

I wash my hands in innocence, and
go about your altar, O Lord.

— Psalm 26:6, NIV

FIFTY-EIGHT

"IF YOU LOVED ME, THEN YOU WOULD—"

Most people lookout for number one. There are those who love to take advantage of innocence. They want to kill it. And whenever you feel dirty around someone, do not let your guard down. Trust the vibes. Love never violates innocence. It rediscovers it. It keeps innocence alive.

Pressured love is not true love. Innocent love never puts its hands where it shouldn't. Innocence never says, "If you really loved me, then you would. . ."

Innocence is yours to lose. And there will be those who will try to steal it. Be smart. "Look straight ahead, and fix your eyes on what lies before you. Mark out a straight path for your feet; then stick to the path and stay safe. Don't get sidetracked; keep your feet from following evil" (Proverbs 4:25-27, NLT).

> When a girl ceases to blush, she has lost the
> most powerful charm of her beauty.
> — *Gregory I*

I will sing and make music with all my soul.

~ ☼ ~

— *Psalm 108:1, NIV*

FIFTY-NINE
MUSIC IS THE LANGUAGE OF THE SOUL

Music feeds something in the soul. It can be anger or love. It can be peace or war. Everyone listens to what feeds their soul. Those who are angry listen to angst artists with a heavy metal thump. Those who are filled with puppy love listen to Hilary Duff or some such artist. And maybe you have been trying to get away from the fury you feel inside. One good way is to ditch the angry music. Stop listening to music that feeds your rage. Find the kind of music that lifts you up.

Be aware of what you feed your soul. You can become malnourished on the wrong music. It is hard to understand how music affects the soul, but it does. Switch up music and see how it affects you. You may be surprised.

Music inflames temperament.
— *Jim Morrison*

Then the Lord said, "If they do not believe you or pay attention to the first miraculous sign, they may believe the second."

— *Exodus 4:8, NIV*

SIXTY
How to Win Back Your Parent's Trust

When you break the rules, you break trust. And you cannot afford that. There are too many places to go to have fun. And being grounded is not one of them. To win back trust you will have to change your attitude and behavior. Moses had to prove he could be trusted as a messenger of God, not once but twice.

Do not be surprised when your parent's are still skeptical after your first sign of repentance. Remorse is what they want to see. But fake tears will not get you out of the house. So think in this way. Ask yourself this question before you make another mistake: "Is this situation helping build back trust or tearing it down?"

How you answer this question will define how much you are to be trusted. Get it right, and you will get your life back.

> Responsibility is the thing people dread most of all.
> Yet it is the one thing in the world that develops us,
> gives us manhood or womanhood fiber.
> — *Frank Crane*

But I tell you that anyone who looks at a woman lustfully has already committed adultery with her in his heart.

— *Matthew 5:28, NIV*

SIXTY-ONE
WHAT IS LUST, REALLY?

Thoughts happen. You cannot stop them. Neurons in your brain will fire and emotions feed off thoughts. They can be triggered when you least expect it. We are attached to the opposite sex. It's natural.

Jesus knew hot-blooded men will lust. But what shocks about this verse is the indictment of "looking." Everybody looks. So does that mean everybody commits adultery with their eyes?

The difference between a dirty thought and a beautiful one is what you do with it. Having a beautiful thought is not a sin. God made beauty and we recognize it. But if you take that thought to the next level and think, *I wish I could—* Then you have crossed over into lust. Lust happens when we change a beautiful thought into a dirty little wish.

> Before a man gives way to his passions, even if his thoughts mount an assault against him, he is always a free man in his own city and he has God as an ally.
> — *St. Dorotheos of Gaza*

But Lord, be merciful to us, for we have waited for you. Be our strength each day and our salvation in times of trouble.

— *Isaiah 33:2, NLT*

SIXTY-TWO

HOW TO PUT SOME SNAP, CRACKLE, POP
INTO YOUR MORNING

God knows you are busy. He sees the schedule you keep. He understands the load and the demands upon your time. But you should never be too busy for Him. And this is why the prayer in Isaiah is so relevant. Prayer is fuel for the soul. It is like pulling up to a gas pump. We get filled with the awareness of God. We get filled with His presence. And when we fail to gas up, we feel sluggish. We get overwhelmed by the slightest problem. But when we pray, God meets our need.

Write this verse on an index card. Then tape it to your mirror. Every morning, while you get ready for school, pray it. Ask God to treat you with kindness. Ask Him to be there for you when things go bad. Put your hope in Him. This will put some snap, crackle, pop into your morning. And you will feel energized all day.

> Do not pray for tasks equal to your powers.
> Pray for power equal to your tasks.
> — *Phillips Brooks*

I knew you before I formed you in your mother's womb. Before you were born I set you apart and appointed you as my spokesman to the world.

— *Jeremiah1:5, NLT*

SIXTY-THREE
THE PLAN GOD HAS FOR YOU

We come into the world crying because there is no humor in the birthing room. Think of the whole scene—all of those weird-looking people in pajamas and masks, yelling our name. Then there are the lights, the camera, the action. And behind the camera our father is shooting footage that shakes like the Blair Witch Project. And being born naked is bad enough, but then the scissors cut our only link to the womb. Safety is gone with one snip. Who wouldn't cry?

We can search a lifetime for the safety we felt in the womb. But we were not created for the womb only. We were created to be inside God's plan. Before we saw the light of the birthing room, before we smelled the nurse's coffee breath and felt her cold hands, God kept late hours. He sat at his drawing table and conceived our plan. And the only way to feel safe in this world is to pray, " 'O Lord.' I say, 'You are my place of refuge. You are all I really want in life' " (Psalm 142:5, NLT).

A ship in harbor is safe, but that is not what ships are built for.
— *John A. Shedd*

So let us come boldly to the throne of our gracious God. There we will receive his mercy, and we will find grace to help us when we need it.

— *Hebrews 4:16, NLT*

SIXTY-FOUR
GRACE IS A PARAMEDIC

Grace is a paramedic in an ambulance. It is help in a time of need. And maybe today you feel parched in your soul. It takes place when we choose sin over love for God.

When we increase our sins and seek no forgiveness, our soul becomes a dry place. "They have forsaken me—the fountain of living water." (Jeremiah 2:13, NLT) And if you feel dry, ask for grace. But remember, it is not cheap, this grace. The sin it heals and the "fresh flowing waters" it brings are accounted for and charged just like a hospital bill. And someone has to pay when you can't. So the bill gets nailed onto outstretched Hands. On His brow the debt rests. In Christ's death the bill is paid. And just because we can find grace in the desert, does not mean it is cheap. It cost Jesus His life.

> Like any other gift, the gift of grace can be
> yours only if you'll reach out and take it.
> — *Frederick Buechner*

From there Elisha went up to Bethel. As he was walking along the road, some youths came out of the town and jeered at him. "Go on up, you baldhead!" they said. "Go on up, you baldhead!" He turned around, looked at them and called down a curse on them in the name of the Lord. Then two bears came out of the woods and mauled forty-two of the youths.

— *2 Kings 2:23-24, NIV*

SIXTY-FIVE

TEENS DEVOURED BY BEARS AFTER LAUGHING AT BALD MAN!

Bald heads are funny to some people. Sure, some people try to cover them up. Some buy rugs. Some have wrap around jobs. These can be hilarious, especially when the wind blows. But we have to respect men with bald heads. They are giving God a break. Did you know God counts the number of hairs on our head (Matthew 10:30)?

Maybe God created a bald head on a Friday. It was quitting time, and still there were heads of hair to count. So he decided, "Let's just shave their heads." Maybe God needed a break. This could be a possibility. But this does not mean He is laughing. If anything, He hurts. And He pays back those who jest at someone else's expense. This is why two bears came out of the woods and devoured forty-two of the youth. They made fun of Elisha's bald head. And in the end, it was no laughing matter. Who knows, could it happen again?

Scoff not at the natural defects of any which are not in their power to amend. It is cruel to beat a cripple with his own crutches!

— *Thomas Fuller*

Let us behave decently, as in the daytime, not in orgies and drunkenness, not in sexual immorality and debauchery, not in dissension and jealousy.

— *Romans 13:13, NIV*

SIXTY-SIX
VIRGINITY IS NOT A CURSE

Being a virgin doesn't make you a freak. It is a badge of honor that you will give your future spouse. So never lose sight of your wedding day. It will happen.

The way to remain a virgin is to make a commitment right now. You cannot wait until you are tempted. Psychologists have proven that at the moment of attraction and flirtation our bodies, minds, and reasoning are temporarily held hostage to the impulsive parts of our brains. Meaning, you will have a hard time making a rational decision when tempted. This is why having your mind made up about staying a virgin is critical. Go buy a purity ring. It is a tangible reminder that you have made a pledge to God. Then use common sense.

Keep your promise.

> Conscience is the inner voice which warns us
> that someone may be looking.
> — *H.L. Mencken*

Owls of many kinds will live among the ruins of its palaces, hooting from the gaping windows. Rubble will block all the doorways, and the cedar paneling will lie open to the wind and weather.

— Zephaniah 2:14, NLT

SIXTY-SEVEN
WHAT TO DO WITH YOUR DEEP SECRET

Not everyone has seen an owl. But most have heard one. Its hoot usually comes in present darkness. But in this verse the owl is in the window. He hoots for all to see. And he is not a ghastly-looking creature. His eyebrows are wicked. So are the eyes beneath. But the light does him a justice that darkness hides.

When our darkness is revealed, when that place in our soul becomes light, we discover it is not so bad. Left in darkness the devil will use it against us. He says, "Others will think you are a bad person. You better keep it hidden." But this is not true. When we trust Satan with a secret, we become his slave. But sins exposed to the light will no longer have a hold over us. Remember, a day is coming when "He will bring to light what is hidden in darkness and will expose the motives of men's hearts" (1 Corinthians 4:5, NIV). So shine light into your darkness.

He who trusts secrets to a servant makes him his master.
— *John Dryden*

The son said to him, "Father, I have sinned against heaven and against you. I am no longer worthy to be called your son."

— *Luke 15:21, NIV*

SIXTY-EIGHT
What to Do When You Are Stuck

People get stuck. We get stuck in elevators, stuck on runways, stuck in traffic, even stuck in sin. We convince ourselves that God does not want us anymore. So we remain broken. But in the parable of the prodigal son we discover God's nature toward sinners.

The son took his inheritance and blew it in Las Vegas. He played every sin he could uncover. But the money ran out. And his so-called friends deserted him. Then hunger set in. So he took a job slopping hogs. And he ate some of the slop himself. It was Fear Factor contestant food. Then he came to his senses. He got out of the rut and went home. And he begged his father to make him a servant. But his father welcomed him home as a son. Then the father threw a bash, a "Forgiveness Party!" And so it is with God. We can get unstuck and go home to Him. He is always waiting for his wayward children.

Forgiveness is the remission of sins. For it is by this that what has been lost, and was found, is saved from being lost again.
— *St. Augustine*

For it is commendable if a man bears up under the pain of unjust suffering because he is conscious of God.

— *1 Peter 2:19, NIV*

SIXTY-NINE

WHY BAD THINGS HAPPEN TO GOOD PEOPLE

Life is difficult. Most days it makes no sense. People we love get cancer. Our friends die in car wrecks. And life seems so random and hard to understand. Why doesn't God do something about pain and evil? Why does He allow bad things to happen to good people?

No one can really say for sure. Some say it is because God has given us free will. And because of this free will some people choose evil. Sinful people cross our path and wreak havoc. This is hard to understand. Others say the only other alternative is for God to make us robots. Then He would have complete control. But who wants that?

The solution for the problem of pain and evil is to understand that God became its victim. He solved the problem by allowing His Son to be killed. He knows the pain of it. And He also knows the victory over it. And so will we. So do not be mad at God. He gave His all.

> Try to exclude the possibility of suffering which the order of nature and the existence of free wills involve, and you find that you have excluded life itself.
>
> — *C.S. Lewis*

Suddenly, Jesus himself came along and joined them and began walking beside them. But they didn't know who he was, because God kept them from recognizing him. "You seem to be in a deep discussion about something," he said. "What are you so concerned about?" They stopped short, sadness written across their faces.

— Luke 24:15-17, NLT

SEVENTY
LIFE CAN GET CONFUSING SOMETIMES

W hat you are becoming is not what you want to be. It is not you. Deep inside you know this. But right now you are confused. It happens. It happened to two men on the road to Emmaus. They were trying to work it all out in their minds. The events surrounding Jesus' death didn't make sense. The past was making the future uncertain. But in their confusion Christ could be found. For doubt is the threshold of true faith. This is how we get back on the right road. We have to doubt the one we are on. And if you ever find yourself lost in a distant country, make a change. Come home. All you have to do is talk to Him. Tell Him what is bothering you. Put your doubt out in the open.

The two men discovered more than a mere traveler. They found Christ in the midst of their confusion. So can you.

> It requires wisdom to understand wisdom:
> the music is nothing if the audience is deaf.
> — *Walter Lippman*

This man lived in the tombs, and no one could bind him any more, not even with a chain. For he had often been chained hand and foot, but he tore the chains apart and broke the irons on his feet. No one was strong enough to subdue him. Night and day among the tombs and in the hills he would cry out and cut himself with stones.

— *Mark 5:2; 4-5, NLT*

SEVENTY-ONE
SELF-MUTILATION

The demoniac was a throwaway person. And society had tossed. They chained him hand and foot. But he broke the chains. He streaked naked in the quiet valley below. And scars were his only dress. They covered him like dirt, making him feel cheap inside. So he cut. "Night and day among the tombs and in the hills he would cry out and cut himself with stones" (Mark 5:5, NIV). And whatever cutting did for him, it didn't help matters. He still hated himself. And there weren't enough stones in the Middle East to make it go away. There was only One who could help, only One who could take the pain away.

Cutting never takes away the pain. It only damages the skin beyond repair. And there will come a point when you will go too far. God does not want that, and neither do you. Get help. Talk to someone.

It is necessary to the happiness of a man
that he be mentally faithful to himself.
— *Thomas Paine*

Then I turned my thoughts to consider wisdom, and also madness and folly.

~ ☼ ~

— *Ecclesiastes 2:12, NIV*

SEVENTY-TWO
WHY DO WE LISTEN TO MADNESS?

Madness, who can trust it? Why give it our thoughts? Why listen when it tells us we are broken? "You are beyond repair," is what it says. But like the dog returning to its vomit, somehow madness entices us to come back—back to the thoughts of despair. Back to the belittling comments in the mirror. Back to the voice in the lunchroom, "You're too fat to eat. Plus, you're ugly. Everybody hates you. I hate you."

Madness has its way of sounding like Mom, like friends, like us at times. It makes us hate life. We get so tired of keeping up a smiling face, so tired of trying to please this belittling voice. But what makes madness go away? We refuse to listen. We fix our thoughts on what is true and honorable and right (Philippians 4:8, NLT). And the truth is madness is a liar. Satan is an accuser. Whenever we make accusations against ourselves, it is not the Spirit of God. God builds up, not tears down.

> When a man lives with God, his voice shall be as sweet
> as the murmur of the brook and rustle of the corn.
> — *Ralph Waldo Emerson*

On the first day, Jonah started into the city. He proclaimed: "Forty more days and Nineveh will be overturned."

— *Jonah 3:4, NIV*

SEVENTY-THREE
How to Take a Do-Over

Jonah ran from God. At first, he went in the opposite direction, away from God's plan. He paid his own fare and boarded a boat headed for Tarshish. And anytime we run from God, we pay our own way. And Jonah ran in his own strength, in his own way and got swallowed by a whale. Then he became bile on the beach. Wrung out and depleted. This is when he made the best choice of his life. He repented and turned around.

It may be the darkest moment of your life. There's an old saying: "It's always the darkest before the dawn." So you may be in the best place of your life. Jonah was. He was in the dark side of a whale's belly, but then he experienced the "first day" of light. "He started into the city." And, oh, how great he must have felt. He was back on the path of God's plan.

Jonah took a do-over. So can you!

> It is no disgrace to start all over.
> It is usually an opportunity.
> — *George Matthew Adams*

D o everything without complaining or arguing . . .

~ ✪ ~

— *Philippians 2:14, NIV*

SEVENTY-FOUR
BICKERING IN THE TRENCHES OF HOME LIFE

It's clear to everyone but them. Do they hate each other? Why can't they just stop fighting? Every night the same routine—he drinks his beer and she gives up on him. But then, as if their fighting has its own cycle, they brighten in anger and start fresh again.

Marriages will have their spats. This is normal. But when it becomes an everyday occurrence, something is wrong. And maybe they need to know. They need to know they are making us crazy, making us want to run and hide. We create distractions to escape. We stay busy. Or, we just stay away. But this never seems to help, because eventually we have to go home, eventually the cycle has to be broken. We have to say, "I will not be them one day." This is a goal, an obtainable one. But maybe they do not know they are hurting the family. So it's okay to tell them how we feel. We can't give up on them.

> A marriage without conflicts is almost as
> inconceivable as a nation without crises.
> — *André Maurois*

You were running a good race.
Who cut in on you and kept
you from obeying the truth?

~ ~

— Galatians 5:7, NIV

SEVENTY-FIVE

HOW TO WIN SELF-RESPECT AND POPULARITY

Some so-called friends will try to get you off course. Wrong roads look good in the beginning. At the corner of every wayward road is a signpost that reads, "You will find popularity here." So we travel that way. We abandon our heart's warning. And temptation is nothing more than a detour down a dead-end street. Most of the time we do not realize it until we get snared. And sometimes we have to make a split-second decision to avoid trouble. Know this—the easy road to popularity is not always the best road. You must do the hard work of obeying the part of you that says, "No!"

We get off course when we try to please everyone but God. So always stop at the crossroads of temptation and ask this question: "Will doing this really make me popular or will this get me in trouble?" And no one can make the decision but you. Choose wisely and you win more than popularity. You win self-respect, and this can be very popular.

I am tied to the stake, and I must stand the course.
— *William Shakespeare*

D o not judge, or you too will be judged.

~ ☼ ~

— *Matthew 7:1, NIV*

SEVENTY-SIX
How Not to Be Judged by Others

Not all cheerleaders are egomaniacs. Most jocks can spell Mississippi, even if they cannot point it out on a map. And nerds? Well, they are people too. So what if they have a pocket liner? Who cares if tape holds their glasses together? It may mean they are poor. For the poor will always be with us. They will have clothes to match their poverty. So do not judge a group of people based upon labels. Inside every group are people just like you. They got up this morning and put eyeliner on one eye at a time. They brushed their teeth, just like you. Okay, most of them brushed their teeth.

Every youth group, every church, every school will contain people who get on your nerves. Try not to label them. Be nice to everyone. You will win favor with God and your enemies. People will say, "You are different." Long to hear this. "Make it your ambition to lead a quiet life, to mind your own business . . . so that your daily life may win the respect of outsiders" (1 Thessalonians 4:11-12, NIV).

All men are not cast in the same mold.
— *American Proverb*

And all of us have had that veil removed so that we can be mirrors that brightly reflect the glory of the Lord.

— *2 Corinthians 3:18, NLT*

SEVENTY-SEVEN

COSMETIC SURGERY IS NOT BEAUTY DIVINE

The mirror is where we go to wage war with imperfections. We pluck our eyebrows. We scope out zits on our face. We hate the way our nose looks. But the "mirror, mirror on the wall" is not where you find true beauty. The beauty of a person is how they reflect to others the glory of the Lord. People notice this. Because when we reflect the Lord, our imperfections don't go away, but they fade. They dim in the light of His glory on our face.

The way to get the Lord's glory on your face is to remove the mask. Let people see who you really are on the inside. Let them see your strong faith. Let them know where you stand on issues. It will reflect an inner magnificence. And don't be surprised when people ask you what has changed. "Did you get plastic surgery?" they might ask. If they do, tell them beauty goes deeper than that.

Never purchase beauty products in a hardware store.
— Miss Piggy

You can enter God's Kingdom only through the narrow gate. The highway to hell is broad, and its gate is wide for the many who choose the easy way.

— *Matthew 7:13, NLT*

SEVENTY-EIGHT

THE GIMMICK OF FOLLOWING GOD
IN YOUR SPARE TIME

Gimmicks abound. There is one for spot removal and one for pain. Then there are those that will make you rich. But don't fall for gimmicks. You cannot get buns of steel while wiggling your toe. Abs only get buff by doing stomach crunches. Nothing comes easy, except zits.

To lose weight you have to work at it. There are no secret little pills. And the same goes with God. To get close to God it will take more than spare time. The Apostle Paul believes we should pray instead of worry. "Don't worry about anything; instead, pray about everything. Tell God what you need, and thank him for all he has done" (Philippians 4:6, NLT). And this could take all day and a lifetime.

There are no gimmicks when it comes to following God. He demands from us our all.

> I know God will not give me anything I can't handle.
> I just wish that He didn't trust me so much.
> — *Mother Theresa*

So don't get tired of doing what is good. Don't get discouraged and give up, for we will reap a harvest of blessing at the appropriate time.

— *Galatians 6:9, NLT*

SEVENTY-NINE
LIFE IS NOT A GAME

Some people can't stand to lose. There is nothing wrong with wanting to win. But life is not a game. It is not a competitive struggle to see who has all the beauty or gets to be valedictorian. Competitive people attach their identity to how well they do. Never tie your identity to how you look or what you wear or what someone thinks about both. Your identity does not come from being better than the rest. It comes from what Christ thinks about you. Be concerned more about what He thinks than what others think. Then you will find your public image really does not matter. Everyone likes someone who has peace within. They are drawn to it, because if they spilled their guts, they would admit that you have what they are really looking for. So don't get tired of doing what is good. We get a reward in the end.

Discouragement is the opposite of courage.
— *Connie Tilley*

Jacob replied, "First sell me your birthright."

"Look, I am about to die," Esau said.

"What good is the birthright to me?"

But Jacob said, "Swear to me first."

So he swore an oath to him, selling his birthright to Jacob. Then Jacob gave Esau some bread and some lentil stew. He ate and drank, and then got up and left. So Esau despised his birthright.

— *Genesis 25:31-34, NIV*

EIGHTY

What You Get in the Spur of the Moment

This is one of the worst trades in history. Esau traded his birthright for stew. What was he thinking? He was thinking of the moment. He was thinking about stew. He was thinking about making the pangs of hunger go away. It was a trade in the moment of weakness.

And we make these trades everyday. We trade our peace for the worry of this world. We trade love for hate. We trade our inner hope for doubt. We doubt we are good enough. We doubt we will make it. Esau doubted he would make it. He said forget the birthright, I'm about to die. I want stew now! And even Eve made a dumb trade. She traded paradise for a piece of fruit. It got her kicked out of the garden. So make wise trades. Never make a decision based on a spur of the moment lust. No matter how strong the attraction, it is a dumb trade.

When you have learned how to decide with God
all decisions become as easy and as right as breathing.
— *Unknown*

If your gift is to encourage others, do it! If you have money, share it generously. If God has given you leadership ability, take the responsibility seriously. And if you have a gift for showing kindness to others, do it gladly.

— *Romans 12:8, NLT*

EIGHTY-ONE
WHAT IT MEANS TO BE A LEADER

A leader is someone who others want to follow and imitate. They start fashion trends and set the pace. They establish mood. They lead others to Christ by their actions. They are not swayed by mob psychology that says, "Everybody is doing it, so must I."

Leaders never make decisions based on what others are doing. Leaders believe they have what it takes to succeed. They externalize their problems, meaning they never get down on themselves. They see difficulty as a hurdle that can be jumped. They never tell themselves, "I do not have what it takes." They take what they have and attempt great things. A leader believes the Apostle Paul's creed: "For I can do everything with the help of Christ who gives me the strength I need" (Philippians 4:13, NLT).

Be a leader! Never follow the crowd and shipwreck your faith. Your school is looking for someone to look up to. So why not be the one who leads.

> The hardest struggle of all is to be something
> different from what the average man is.
> — *Robert H. Schuller*

For the wages of sin is death,
but the free gift of God is eternal life
through Christ Jesus our Lord.

— *Romans 6:23, NLT*

EIGHTY-TWO
What to Do with Sin

Life is one big spot broken into particles. There are ink spots, blood spots, and spots on a dog. Then there are sunspots and spots on the windshield that used to be bugs. And some spots are good spots. Then other ones have to be removed, like the black spot on our soul called sin. It is our plague—an emptiness that will not go away. It is a spot that cannot be removed with Comet and elbow grease. Mere human means are not enough. It takes something larger than the Universe. This is why Christ died on the Cross. He paid the debt for our sins. He died in our place. And now all we have to do to remove the black spot of sin is to believe. We must believe that Christ is God. That He died for our sins and rose again on the Third Day. Then we have to ask Him to forgive our sins, to come inside, to help us with the spot each day.

> Sins cannot be undone, only forgiven.
> — *Igor Stravinsky*

In everything you do, stay away from complaining and arguing, so that no one can speak a word of blame against you.

— Philippians 2:14-15, NLT

EIGHTY-THREE
How to Deal with Crybabies

People who whine seek attention. They do not want solutions. They want you to feel sorry for them. And when some crisis gets more attention than theirs, they will act out in new and more theatrical ways. They will criticize the other crisis. They will say, "That's nothing. You should hear what happened to me this morning."

Whiners are also blamers. They blame everything and everybody for their troubles. So when they blame you, do not respond. It is not your responsibility. You are their friend not their scapegoat. It may take awhile but sooner or later they will get the message. And when they do they will start to grow up.

Even the lion has to defend himself against flies.
— *Anonymous*

Therefore, since we are surrounded by such a great cloud of witnesses, let us throw off everything that hinders and the sin that so easily entangles, and let us run with perseverance the race marked out for us.

— Hebrews 12:1-2, NIV

EIGHTY-FOUR
HEY, YOU! GET OFF MY CLOUD!

Clouds sail and break apart. They run the gamut of all rain storms and even carry no rain at all. So when Hebrews talks about a "cloud of witnesses," what does it mean? Most likely it means we look to those saints who have gone before us. Their obedience spurs us on. And each of us have different "witnesses"—those who encourage us—on our clouds. During our lifetime there will be those who will get off and those who will get on.

It could be a father who criticizes you on the playing field. Maybe it is an overbearing, highly critical mother. It could be an arrogant coach, an insensitive peer, an intolerable teacher. The challenge of life is to know how to say, "Hey, you! Get off my cloud!" There are those who do not belong there.

Learn to keep the saints of old on your cloud. Follow their example. Endure hardships, but do not let critical people put you out of the race.

God does not require of you what is beyond your ability, what leads you away from God, or what makes you depressed or sad.
— Henri Nouwen

Once when Jesus had been out praying, one of his disciples came to him as he finished and said, "Lord, teach us to pray, just as John taught his disciples."

— *Luke 11:1, NLT*

EIGHTY-FIVE
How to Pray to Know God's Will

The disciples did not ask the secrets of turning water into wine. They did not want the recipe for turning stones into bread. It was prayer they desired. And this reveals Jesus' power in its fullest. He was never more like God than when He prayed. "Anyone who has seen me has seen the Father" (John 14:9, NIV).

When you pray, ask God for direction. You probably won't hear a loud voice or even a whisper. But prayer aligns our will with God's. It is the act of letting go. And selfishness is half of the battle we face. We want to do things our way. We want to control God's timetable. This is why we never find God's will. But the moment we trust God, we are never more like His Son. "Trust in the Lord with all your heart and lean not on your own understanding; in all your ways acknowledge him, and he will make your paths straight" (Proverbs 3:5-6, NIV).

> How can I say that I have found Him and found myself in Him if I never know Him or think of Him, never take any interest in Him or seek Him or desire His presence in my soul?
> — *Thomas Merton*

From the heavens the stars fought, from their courses they fought against Sisera.

— *Judges 5:20, NIV*

EIGHTY-SIX
"The Emmy Goes To—"

Sometimes it feels like the stars of heaven are fighting against us. Nothing ever seems to go right. We feel cursed. Everyone else has all the luck. They have riches. We are poor. We seem underprivileged. Everyone else has the power of fashion behind them. It's as if the stars of heaven are fighting against us, labeling us unworthy of love, unworthy of attention. When we feel this way, we are making ourselves the lead actor/actress and the world our stage. And life focused on us will always feel cursed. But remember that God is not obligated to make us happy at His expense. This is center stage thinking. So instead of aligning yourself with your own stars, align yourself with the God who made them.

Life doesn't seem so cursed when we make this life about Him. We do this by submitting. We do this by learning how to follow. We do this by stepping off center stage, making God the lead actor. Then we become a supporting role. And who knows, we might win an Emmy.

Self conceit may lead to self destruction.
— *Aesop*

Then the Lord said to Cain, "Why are you angry?
Why is your face downcast? If you do what is right,
will you not be accepted? But if you do not do
what is right, sin is crouching at your door;
it desires to have you, but you must master it."

— *Genesis 4:6-7, NIV*

EIGHTY-SEVEN
THERE'S SOMETHING CROUCHING AT YOUR DOOR

It crouches at the door. Do not go look. It is there. It's at every door. Sometimes we let it in like a stray cat. We feed it our soul. And this is what it wants. How did it get at everyone's door? "Sin entered the entire human race. Adam's sin brought death, so death spread to everyone, for everyone sinned" (Romans 5:12, NLT). And it crouched at Cain's door. Waiting. Just waiting. And Cain let it in—even though God warned against it.

Cain killed his brother. Then God sent him packing for the city of Nod. And isn't this ironic? The way sin gets inside is by a simple nod, a simple yes or no. But don't despair. Christ can evict it. All you have to do is ask. He will speak to the Father in our defense. He is the atoning sacrifice for the sins of the whole world (1 John 2:1-2). Christ is the answer. He can kick sin out. And once He does, leave it outside. But never forget it crouches at the door.

The confession of evil works is
the first beginning of good works.
— *St. Augustine*

For our struggle is not against flesh and blood, but against the rulers, against the authorities, against the powers of this dark world and against the spiritual forces of evil in the heavenly realms.

— *Ephesians 6:12, NIV*

EIGHTY-EIGHT
THE WAR IN THE HEAVENLY REALMS

We cannot see this war. There are no atomic blasts. No mushroom clouds. No tanks rolling across a desert. But this war is just as real. It is the war for our soul in the heavenly realms. But we have no reason to fear. God is stronger than the forces of destruction. "Nothing can ever separate us from his love. Death can't, and life can't. The angels can't, and the demons can't. Our fears for today, our worries about tomorrow, and even the powers of hell can't keep God's love away" (Romans 8:38, NLT).

The battle belongs to God. Nothing can pluck us from His hand. But fascination with the demonic is Satan's ploy to get our minds off Christ and onto him. It is a distraction. Satan loves to brag about his so-called powers. But who cares about a bunch of demonic losers? Let's keep our focus on God.

> When we lose power with God, we know of a certainty
> that the problem lies within us and not with God.
> — *Ray H. Wood*

*W*hy are you downcast, O my soul? Why so disturbed within me? Put your hope in God, for I will yet praise him.

— *Psalm 42:5, NIV*

EIGHTY-NINE
LISTEN UP!

We can tell ourselves all the wrong things. We say, "I hate myself." "I wish I were dead." "I can't stand to look at myself in the mirror."

We hate ourselves with words and thoughts of despair. And, like David, we have to talk hope into ourselves. "Why are you downcast, O my soul? Look around at those who love you. And don't say you don't have anyone. You do. Look! Can't you see? And always remember that God died for you. If you were the only person on earth, God would have died for you, O my soul."

Speaking to your soul is how you lift your spirits. This is what David did. He instructed his soul. He put his hope in God. So tell your soul what it should be happy about it. And if you cannot think of something to say, just use David's words. And whatever you do, go talk to a counselor. There are people who will listen.

> Have you realized that most of your unhappiness
> in life is due to the fact that you are listening to
> yourself instead of talking to yourself?
> — *D. Martyn Lloyd-Jones*

*W*hen a gentle south wind began to blow, they thought they had obtained what they wanted; so they weighed anchor and sailed along the shore of Crete. Before very long, a wind of hurricane force, called the "northeaster," swept down from the island. The ship was caught by the storm and could not head into the wind; so we gave way to it and were driven along.

— *Acts 27:13-15, NIV*

NINETY

DECEPTIVE WINDS CAN SHIPWRECK YOUR FAITH

It was a nice day. The sun was a fireball just three degrees less than being a scorcher. The water was crystal clear. The beach accepted the tide and shortened its breadth. A crab scurried along, and then disappeared into a hole. Gone was the crab. Gone was the fear of sailing. They had received the breeze they desired. It was a Southern breeze. Its manners were polite. This is why the captain liked it. So he set sail. But a "northeaster" swept across the bridge. It peeled back the captain's hair and the hull of the ship. And it all started with a deceptive wind.

Gentle winds can deceive. Always look down the road, beyond the present moment. Look for where things might end up. If you sense danger, dock the boat. Become a landlubber. Be a geek. "Be as shrewd as snakes and as innocent as doves" (Matthew 10:16, NIV). It will keep you out of trouble.

> Nothing is so difficult as not deceiving oneself.
> — *Ludwig Wittgenstein*

David took these words to heart and was very much afraid of Achish king of Gath. So he pretended to be insane in their presence; and while he was in their hands he acted like a madman, making marks on the doors of the gate and letting saliva run down his beard.

— *1 Samuel 21:12-13, NIV*

NINETY-ONE
When You Come to the End of Yourself

David went insane to escape from the king of Gath. His life was at stake. So he foamed at the mouth and let it dribble into his beard. And this is peculiar behavior. The sane pretends to be insane. Or was it the hand of God leading him? Because God possessed insane people in David's day. So they mistakenly thought. And David wasn't so crazy after all. It was a brilliant move! He reached for the hand of God. He possessed himself with the power he needed to get free. And the king of Gath said, "Look at the man! He is insane! Why bring him to me?" (v. 14)

This may not work today. You could wind up in a psychiatric hospital. But think about this. Next time you find yourself in a particular jam, reach for the power of God. Possess it. Ask God to deliver you. Tell Him you are at your wit's end. God loves to aide those who abandon themselves to Him.

> Without Thee, what am I but a guide
> to my own destruction.
> — *St. Augustine*

It is dangerous to make a rash promise
to God before counting the cost.

— *Proverbs 20:25, NLT*

NINETY-TWO
THINK BEFORE YOU JUMP

Rash decisions make you look like a "heartbreaker." Be careful about breaking someone else's heart. You may discover you want them back. And this waffling back and forth between being in and out of love, may make you permanently "out" with this person. And, others will be afraid to date you. No one wants to be nabbed, and then rejected.

Take some time. Get beyond emotional reasoning, which says, "I feel love so it must be true." Or "I don't feel love so it must not be true." Do not gauge a relationship by how you "feel" in the moment. It's a bad habit, and it can damage your marriage later. In marriage you will not always "feel" in love. This is why we make vows. This is why we say, "For richer or for poorer." Because, when you are poor, love doesn't "feel" so good. It stinks. So learn to take commitments seriously. If you can't, then wait on dating for awhile.

> Better to light a candle than to curse the darkness.
> — *Chinese Proverb*

Will merchants try to buy it?
Will they sell it in their shops?

— *Job 41:6, NLT*

NINETY-THREE
FINDING YOUR BRAND AT THE MALL

The Mall has what you want—The Gap, Gadzooks, and American Eagle. Old Navy too. They can accentuate your positives. They can add lift and slim down. They can even give you a figure if you do not have one. But what can't be bought at the Mall is character. You can't hide it or fluff it up. Everyone knows who the loose girls are. They know the guys who are players. You can get a reputation. You can wear a label. And the thing you want to avoid is becoming a brand at the Mall. People know the labels and will see to it that you get one. You think they do not see. But they do. Character has a hard time concealing itself. It's like a zit. It will keep rising to the surface.

> Character is what you are in the dark.
> — *Dwight Moody*

We are fools for Christ . . .

~ ☼ ~

— 1 Corinthians 4:10, NIV

NINETY-FOUR
A SHIP OF FOOLS

A Ship of Fools exists. The rudder has been torn away. The sea pitches it into danger's grasp. But deep in the hull is peace. No Dramamine needed here. As Nathan O'Neal sings, "Jesus has never been on a boat that wouldn't float." So why do you feel like you are sinking? Yes, it is a Ship of Fools, but there is none like it. The rudder is missing because fools cannot get where they are going. They will end up in the Bermuda Triangle every time. Lost. Missing in action. Overwhelmed and seasick.

And if Christianity is anything, then it is the "All Aboard!" It is the call to load up with the rest of those who are daring enough to be called "fools for Christ." And they say the church is a ship of fools headed off into its own oblivion. But even if that were true, I would rather be a fool for Christ than a damned fool any day.

> Real happiness is cheap enough,
> yet how dearly we pay for its counterfeit.
> — *Hosea Ballou*

For since the creation of the world God's invisible qualities—his eternal power and divine nature—have been clearly seen, being understood from what has been made, so that men are without excuse.

— *Romans 1:20, NIV*

NINETY-FIVE
Do We Have a Chance?

How did the universe begin? I'm sure there is a scientific explanation. But why spend a lifetime trying to prove what we already know. The devil would love to send us on a life search for the meaning of the Universe. He does not want you to come to any conclusions. And it is fun to study black holes and the Milky Way. There is nothing wrong with discussing why life may exist on other planets. But science cannot explain the origin of the Universe. It just can't. Neither will it call God the Creator. It leaves things up for chance, which means we are alone, without our God. If this is true, we don't have a chance. We die. The end. There has to be more than that . . . doesn't it?

> Using the same old materials of earth,
> air, fire, and water, every twenty-four hours
> God creates something new out of them.
> — *Frederick Buechner*

Friend against friend spreads malicious gossip.

— Jeremiah 9:4, NIV

NINETY-SIX
STAYING OUT OF AN INSTANT MESSAGE FIGHT

AIM is a way to stay connected. But sometimes being connected means being in a fight. It is easy to hide behind a screen. It is easy to accuse and put people down. To your face, most of these conversations will not take place. So do not get into an AIM fight. Tell them you would love to get together and talk. People are not so brave when you draw them out from behind the screen.

Make this rule: I will not spread rumors or gossip or accuse others while online. Neither will I respond to those who say I have.

Keep your chat sessions clean of malicious talk and accusations. Remember, people are braver behind a screen. So draw them out. Never go to battle on their terms. You will lose.

> An expert gossiper knows how much
> to leave out of a conversation.
> — *Unknown*

Josiah was eight years old when he became king,
and he reigned in Jerusalem thirty-one years.

— *2 Chronicles 34:1, NIV*

NINETY-SEVEN
WHERE TO FIND THE HELP YOU NEED

Josiah wore Nikes beneath his royal robe. He ate King Vitamin for breakfast and a peanut-butter-and-jelly sandwich for lunch. And he carried a tremendous burden. At age eight, he became king. Then he turned thirteen. And the skating rink was not fun anymore, besides no one would dare race him. So at thirteen, he began to seek the God of David. He wanted his life to matter. So he cleaned up the inner-city. He raided "sex-and-religion shrines" (v.3). He placed more policemen on the beat and posted "Neighborhood Watch" signs to detour crime. Then, at the age of eighteen, he rebuilt the temple and discovered the Book of the Law. It had been missing for years. So they gathered in the temple and renewed their vows to follow God.

Maybe you want your life to make a difference. The key is found in your Bible. Go dig it out. Rediscover it. Josiah did. And he turned his nation back to God.

> If we live good lives, the times are also good.
> As we are, such are the times.
> — *St. Augustine*

I thought, "Those who are older should speak,
for wisdom comes with age."

— *Job 32:7, NLT*

NINETY-EIGHT
HAVING PARENTS CAN BE DANGEROUS

Parents can seem old and dangerous. They can harm a person's image. Who wants to be associated with people who talk about cholesterol and constipation? Who wants to go to Target with the man who sticks his arm in the free blood pressure checker beside the pharmacy? And after the armband has deflated, so has your cool. It can damage your image to be seen with old fogies. But every dog has his day and so will you. You will walk the Mall for exercise. You will swing your arms and be glad you do not have colon cancer. You will constantly call your children and leave overwrought messages on their voicemail. Then you will start to dribble and need Depend undergarments. And maybe you will lose your mind and call your son by your dog's name. You might even forget where you parked the car in Wal-Mart's parking lot. Things can happen when you get old and senile. So be nice to old people. You will be one someday.

> The first sign of maturity is the discovery that
> the volume knob also turns to the left.
> — *Jerry M. Wright*

On the contrary: "If your enemy is hungry, feed him; if he is thirsty, give him something to drink. In doing this, you will heap burning coals on his head."

— *Romans 12:20, NIV*

NINETY-NINE
HOW TO GET BACK AT MEAN GIRLS

Girls can be mean. They can tear you down by attacking your appearance. Girls know how to pick fights. They can settle them too. They know how to kick and gouge and scratch. But do not let things get this far. Fighting mean girls is not an option. You can get them off your back by being nice to them. This will shock their hatred. It is hard to be mean when someone is not being mean back. The payoff of being mean is to see pain on the victim's face. And when you allow them to upset you, it keeps it stirred up. But when nice meets mean, nice will eventually win out. This is the Apostle Paul's point. Heaping coals is not eternal damnation. It is a reality for now. It will cause them to feel shame. But when you fight back, they will feel rage.

So get out there and be nice.

> I will not allow any man to make me
> lower myself by hating him.
> — *Booker T. Washington*

Then he turned toward the woman and said to Simon, "Do you see this woman? I came into your house. You did not give me any water for my feet, but she wet my feet with her tears and wiped them with her hair."

— *Luke 7:44, NIV*

ONE-HUNDRED
WHAT IS A CHURCH?

Jesus let this shady prostitute wash his feet with her tears. He did not yell, "Away from Me, you worker on the corner!" He did not see a label. He saw a human heart reaching out. And He gently and lovingly allowed her to honor Him. And in honoring Him, she poured out all of her sin—every trick she ever turned.

This was the greatest example of the church ever portrayed— sins forgiven and washed away. Heart mended, instead of judged. Tears genuine, not contrived. No dry singing. No dull sermon. It was titled, "Three Ways a Prostitute Can Get Off the Corner."

1) Come to Jesus

2) Fall at His feet

3) Pour out your heart; your tears too.

When the church becomes a den where fake people assemble, then we end up serving a plastic God. And the church becomes the last place to fall on your knees before Him.

We must never serve a plastic god.

It is common for those that are farthest from God,
to boast themselves most of their being near to the Church.
— *Matthew Henry*

ABOUT THE AUTHOR:

Robert Stofel is the author of *God, Are We There Yet?* and *Survival Notes for Graduates.* He is the pastor/planter of Hickory Hills Community Church in Decatur, Alabama. He is a native of Franklin, Tennessee, and for three years he counseled crack addicts in the inner city of Nashville, Tennessee. Stofel is a prolific magazine contributor, and ministers frequently at conferences, such as Youth Encounter in Brisbane, Australia, where he was the keynote speaker. He lives in Alabama with his wife, Jill, and daughters Blair and Sloan.